Michelle Murphy

Disheveled Histories

Wet Cement Press

Berkeley, Asheville, Reno

Disheveled Histories ©2024 by Michelle Murphy
ISBN 979-8-9883840-2-1

Library of Congress Control Number:
2023941912

Cover image:
Sally Reynolds was a Thief (part one)
Courtesy of the artist ©Sheridan Jones

Wet Cement Press
1908 Yolo Ave
Berkeley, CA 94707

www.wetcementpress.com

Acknowledgments

Thank you to the readers and editors of the following journals:

Aeolian Harp—Volume Nine: After All Stay Soft, How to Enough, Task, For the Piano Man Playing on the Side of the Road During the Pandemic

Bangalore Review: Leaving Iowa

Pidgeonholes: How to Fold a Paper Frog

Timber Journal: Honey Drive and Morning Alley

WCP Magazine #1: Tremolo

Contents

How to Fold a Paper Frog

Pain of this season. Some
bit-part of a heart gives
in, a crumbled sentence flattens.
Fold here.

There are cherry bombs
beside cherry pies. Nervous
detonations across the globe.
You mean to go
into this world by yourself?

Fold the top down
along the dotted line. Continue

lifting up. Fold bottom up,
corners down,
create a center.
                    A spring-like prayer,
a loud gong.
That's your life trying to stay.

Wildfire dust blankets
floors, seethes across avenues,
soothsayers read into various faults.
Another end-of-the-world-scenario
smolders this smoked town.

Any live pistol is conditional.
When you let go,
the frog might be triggered
to leap from conception.
Own its motion.
Frog takes on a story of its own.

All this climbing in
and out has made us less
than gorgeous today.
Fold here.

How to Flower

I'm out with lanterns, looking for myself.
—Emily Dickinson

Thousand year roses
exaggerate their fidelity.
Flumped in a jar,
resigned, scent coiled
in folds of dance-fade,

there is no claim
to the body as it confronts
itself in another doorway,
its myopic shadow,
lantern-less,
rigged for slumping
over this year
               as it drops to its knees
without parting its legs.

You don't have to
remember every name
but take mine even
if it lacks audacity.

We used to know
when it was time.
To let ourselves out
before things turned ugly.

When I tore my lip
on the casino floor
a blotchy trail of blood
stained the marble then
disappeared into crimson
and at that very moment a woman
on the slots won big and eyes wide,
screamed to no one in particular,
You rule, black sea, you rule.

How to Enough

"Please control the soul's desire for freedom."
Drones in Shanghai over loudspeaker as people
sing from the balconies during COVID lockdown.

1.

Along lush greens
and flower beds,
stones speak.   Listen as they
find your name ajar
but no longer waiting.

2.

We jimmy history
into place to make
room for us.
If we have no teeth
to barter   say
our names out loud.

3.

Forget this country
of worn wishes.
Stings the scalp and
reckons everything is
nearly lost.

4.

All the letters have been

dropped
here and here,   some softened by rain.

5.

Drink your juice   leave
what is left on the table
next to a hat and empty
briefcase near a typewriter.

Some letters

                    but not enough hours
                    to make a word.

6.

Beached in this
memory that isn't mine
you say we shouldn't talk
for awhile   take in the air
then pass over an orange
from your bag.

7.

In a century of study,
no one has managed
to reinvent gravity.
Insist, instead, for trees
to speak freely.

Task

I read somewhere
about a monk
who gave names
to honeybees.
She understood
lives were short and
thought they shouldn't
die unknown.

If you think about it,
we almost never hear.
What's being said?

Name the ants parading
past the cat bowl and name a spider
haggling for distance.
This sliding door.
Push sound across a rug.
Phish. Hoo.
Pipes tune in a cross-pollinated elegy.

Ahem.
What is the opposite of this year?
What is crime in ordinary language?

A woman makes a peace symbol
in the snow with the heel of her boot.
Next to it, someone traces a gun.
Scrambling eggs in the kitchen,
we are unaware another war has started.

TREMOLO

For my brother, Brett, who jumped off the Golden
Gate Bridge one beautiful March morning.

While the nephew paints with water, the tiger the bear the
elephant, we aren't a circus, he yells into an almost empty
room, and we are startled to be seen. Is this delineation
between water and various heavens, between this family's
yellow wings of disappearance and trails of moonlight left
behind, real? Do you see me?

I'm writing to inform you that the chair you dragged across country, the one always on the verge of devouring itself, recently exploded in a threadbare taxonomy. An implosion, its demise, a belly-up, goose-feather-snowing, thread-flanged vaudeville act. Where are you, my love? Your wheels off, hands no longer shaking at the sight of another sunrise?

Your full name sprawls out beneath my tongue, a body of loose consonants stretched out like a cat or a coil, urging some wild language to unleash itself, become real. Migratory vowels wrench out of a second syllable as you rake air, peel it with your scrawny arms, and for a minute set out in flight. A swift, you say, never settles on the ground. Is a life spent airborne a denial of gravity even if there is no intention of finding home? No chance of ever landing?

It is only a misstep between you and earth as you practice a new aeronautics, one in which you become an unfixed point, wildly gone, almost unbearable in this new cored light, footprints returning from some refracted future. Is this the ancestral pings and pangs we are gifted at birth? Compassion whittled into our ribcage, love, like a thud, fusing us to some beginning we've never practiced?

And now it's been years since your voice hung up on me and sometimes I follow a stranger with a similar gait, or smell your thinning hair in an elevator just emptied. This isn't your responsibility of course, it's my desperation getting in the way. A valley of holograms and echoes I've stuffed into my mouth to keep myself from talking. You know, it's mostly preservation that keeps us forgiving, allows us to continue pouring ourselves into the sea, to drench ourselves in its salt. What else do we have except love's aperture?

Sometimes a dream is more muscle than memory, hours spalled and scribbled, a messy wood we suspend to pinpoint home, an invention of familiar hallways, G-d in the shadows. Even as the body conjures up another tremolo of love, even as bodies begin to soften and crumble, the bird that is our soul takes the enigma (that is us) and breathes into existence the sturdy air, even as it takes our breath away.

There are possibilities, (of course) such as an urge to float under gum-stained water pipes, partially tethered to weeds and willows, the sun like a Dictaphone, taking it all down, recording the river and all its flickers, erasing nothing.

Speak or be silent, you, with your closed arms and disheveled history waiting to be chosen, to be explained plain, feet planted. I've lingered here too long for the chalk, for the blackboard, to show you the map I've made of our lives. It's okay, after all, we are only wolf cubs, blue, blind and deaf, sharpening our teeth on language & its overlap.

How to Talk about Tsunamis

Tell me the one about your boyfriend, just seventeen, shot dead at a gas station in Tennessee in the early morning hours between night and first cold light. Empty fuel can in one hand, faulty flashlight in the other. Light jiggers, switches off and on in shrunken Morse code that might tell us another war is about to begin. Or tell the one where you fall backward into a second cousin's horse trough, rise lustrated, hair thatched in soot and pulpy hay, ready to call the Holy Spirit out from afternoon's unburied shadow. Call to Furies, their supple, fertile wrath. Letting you know this time you've gone too far. Ocular concussion, doctor writes in a yellowed notebook. Had he done such a thing. Had the ink not stained his fingertips. Unapologetic, teeth bared, even Reverend Nightingale can't shut down your substantial homily, its mud dance and sweat.

Or tell the story of my father's mother, her shoulders bent and barbed from riding Greyhound across the middle states, a cornflower blue suitcase & handful of stray English, monosyllables of affection laced to her tongue. What follows is directions on how to boil a chicken, when to skim and rid it of its gray scum float. In lieu of conversation, the sharp continent of her glare settled on your growing stomach, on her son for his delivered lack. His luck, his admitted desire. After a week of sweeping silence under beds, she walks away, not bothering to say goodbye. Screen door swings and swings, rocks gleam in summer's hinged light.

When your water breaks in the town's new bakery, a thick scarf of beer and clotted sugar rises in your nostrils, yeast as a living organism buckles your knees, and mere seconds before you black out, there's this flurried memory of your daddy (he is alive again) loping across the room when you were nine, his mottled-brown arms flapping, imitating a hoot owl. Eyes, dark and wide as an abyss, screeching Hoooo hoooo hoooooo.

BECKONING

After crawling this river
as snakes, as rattle,
I'll comb back your hair,
spit that unruly cowlick
into place
blow off a fine dust that's settled
in your eyebrow's arch.
We'll croon, belly-down,
scratch dirt with our fingers,
spell our names out with sticks.

Today, I lost someone I
knew a long time ago.

Mud is not a forecast.
Mud is neither praise nor pardon.
When the sky shifts,
it's sudden and I keep wishing
for eyes in the back of this skull
to spell out where we've been,
admit us back into the story.

I've been told you
don't have to believe
in prayer in order for
it to work.   An acorn placed here.
A fistful of pine

needles there.
If we ever meet again,
I'll fill my mouth with overripe
berries to watch you laugh,
take your hand as
we thread the redwoods.
Call that too.

Reverse Verification
of Winter

For each commandment
there is a corresponding
limb in the human body.
Reach under the hood
of the cosmos and repair
your ignition, your revolution.

If you give this
detonated nest the
close-up it deserves
you'll find slick feathers,
improbable hope hatching
at the edge of the world.
A future dreaming itself
inside the cracks of an egg.

When tomorrow unfolds
another snowstorm
from another atonal sky,
and the dead letters
wind their way home,
I'll reach for my shovel,
dig in with my hips,
spread mulch over
the filthy snow
to make it look like new.

Leaving Iowa

For my brother, Dean, 1958-1982

In fact, we barely knew your slim thicket
of zip codes could be so easily shrugged
from memory, there wasn't even a backseat side-eye.
We don't belong to this hatched argument
shush baby, Furies sometimes
like to engine up old curses, barb into
every word until they shut up altogether.

September is lodged in my throat
though I'm still not sure why a bunch
of cardboard boxes leaves me
dry-mouthed, craving something cold to sip.

Begin with Iowa, its road leads away
next to a track with no train
near a wave of faded cornstalks
bugs smack the windshield phing phing phong
Crows jangle figure eights above the car
until they grow bored
then it's just us moving from
and to, landing anywhere.

SKUNK WEED

If we wish to compress something, we first must let it fully expand. —*Lao Tzu*

Sometimes my brothers skate by in a drift of flannel, a stank of skunk-weed and misfortune wrecking over their pores as if they're still beyond physics and psychics. Yet no one has any good answers for why one is prone to fail.

& here you are, stepping in for them, another excuse for the constant awol & cheeks that tend to get snagged in rearview mirrors. Glare of gunfire.

Don't give them the satisfaction of reminding them what year it is. Even your mother knows she has to walk these woods alone, carry the length of her shadow from one tree trunk to another, and in time, leave its husk to find another way home.

As for the father of this story, he's understood by his watery blue eyes & stark lack of direction. Blood as a difficult science we wade through, discerning specs and lowdowns, our almost connections.

I've given up on trying to find latitudes & longitudes on this map of inexact perimeters because even if the needle's found there's always a way to shift its position.

Feel free to ask a similar question even as you and I slip in and out of whatever conversation, one where our words are uncomfortable but almost ring true.

WAR MUZAK

Bald mountains wear toupees of late spring snow.
An allegory, an ambush.

Middle: a tender alphabet.
It is a time of flux translations, wrested streets.

Everything is. Discard. Even flute.
Mouth stripped, no longer creates a note.

Past gilded doorways, inside expansive
chambers, sober men talk sideways of their childhoods.

What is stolen & can't be retrieved. Around the next
corner, apples. Where before there was nothing.

CAESURA

Call us creatures
of fume.
Call us battle born
between borders.

Margins of error.
Memory as caesura
we can hang this
ragged spirit on.

Sunlight humbles
over troubled births
and funerals with
the same wide veracity.
We are here to find
a bright way home.

Finches sound their
father's signature
over branches,
warn other birds
of weathers singing
outside the frame
before woods became smoke,
dimming light to a single
wild consonant,
home-brewed,

without context.
Someday, when we clear
this land of its improbable ash,
an alternate ending might appear
& I'll show you my sword.
How it schemes.
Trembles in my hand.

Doctrine of Last Things

Another body is
pulled. Small drown-
shroud, ache-
blue speculation

from the river.
Geese line the banks
like crude teeth.
Not all can be retrieved
from cut shadow.

Night then, is manna.

These rapids spit out
trailer hitch, tangled lures,
dime-size locket, crumbled jacket.
Did you hear as we
cast song after
song from the bridge
last night?
Aiming our throat-song

into eddies?
Today, we are
a quorum of broken stone.
Laments allow us praise.
Let us say.
Sun. Suitcase. Egg.

How to Unfold History

A leap unbroken without landing
isn't quite death either.
Left tethered between
a purgatory of birds,
contingency feathers,
wings unfolded,
in genetic motion.

Even as we grapple
for answers mid-flight,
(what are we now beyond flesh?)
something close
to math suspends
the trigger,
velocity into another

threshold thicket noise
into which you might
lift from this particular
lenticular cloud.
Gleam, buoyant,
un-hemmed,
limber in this
history unfolding.

How To Remember Heat

Sometimes, I walk a trail where ash recently spit, rose, then blanketed the sky. Remnants of charred branch, shorn hills. I am not ready for this wildfire to turn me inside out. For trunks, belly hot, to stand in as temporary signatures.

Today will be the last update for the time being. This slump of loss is embryonic, crammed inside our mouths, amorphous, unformed. Names that were not mine are mine now.

We interrupt this year for an important message. Our hands genuflect, bodies swell as they settle, pencil in dates, numbers, dissected vowels. Our primitive haste to move forward without understanding where we've been.

Define isolated pockets of heat for the audience. Walk these hills and follow the tracks of wild horses, shadows spent, left behind, then a rattlesnake's charred hiss lingering on the edge of itself. Sometimes, your laugh smolders, fills the room where we sit, waiting for the rules of this heat to be explained.

Hospice Tango

Torsion, the twist in the waist, enables the embrace
to remain with the partner, despite the direction in
which the legs go.

"Argentine Tango"—by Thomas Rasche

And to know, soon, birds will fly in torn gossamer flocks, blot out whatever sky. And before that, physicians will enter, efficient and dazzling, attempt to wedge detail between larynx and lung's diminishing probability.

I am moving across the floor backwards. In fray. Embracing myself.

What beautiful effect could define this final curtain, this exit stripped to the core, violoncello in place of double bass, strings wound around my hips, leading me from door to window to baffle in this music?

A low center of gravity is meant to hinge on present tense and ground us to the world.

Do you have a light? A man in a green hospital gown stares down your coat pocket. He has a cigarette tucked behind his ear, his face, a gray afterthought goes on forever.

Somewhere, names rest in a ballroom of uncomfortable chairs, waiting to be called. Or that's what I sometimes believe because there is no shoulder to grasp in this in-between grapple between here and where. No kiss to center this year.

In this artificial light, our faces flicker like a strip of yellowed celluloid. I am new to this rotation, this shift, as you slow-walk your breath forward and turn away.

Byways and One Way Streets

Stranded Way

Left to covet
a stopped watch.
Every hour is
spare. A silk bag
of undone pearls.
Dislocation whittled
inside war's tenacity.

Honey Drive

But how can
we afford this road.
Feedback crash.
Some are strung out
on their own honey.
Trundle waves are
four short chords.
Less than a smoke.
Marvelous air,
scaffolds are being
built for home.

Morning Alley

Who went running
despite all her lame
excuses. Amplify your
boiling. Point
out what depends
on being held.
Meet the ear
at its war, another plan
advances into morning
darkness.

Rain Cul-de-sac

Avoid corridors of those
who pace their voice.
Gold is promised to
those who tread.
Listen to another revision,
other cold rains will fall.

Seed Drive

From the heart's figure,
regardless of its move.
Done with guns,
plant seeds inside pockets.
Fill an unfolded mouth
with this tremble rain.

Bullet Avenue

Snipers are real.
Starched sky in this
fast future.
Spilt in gas, lightning.
Sorrow this tableau.
Even as the ship drains
a harbor trying to stay afloat.

Void Road

Every window closes.
A raccoon is never
ready to fly.
Heal the past. So much
happens in a fools' kiss.
Seeds are sometimes silent.
And even a butterfly
can anger God.

Concatenation

While I quibble with cashiers in fast-food restaurants, or toy with shepherds as they wrestle sheep into makeshift order, death continues to simmer in my belly, and where my breast once was suspended, a cauldron of scars boil over, red, random, spelling nothing of this story.

There comes a time the dead can barely budge from their comfortable chairs. Instead, we should bring them new stories of themselves, share a meal, prove that beyond this page, we are still called, erratic and true.

There are days we stomp thickets and forests, charge at giants with ferocity, dream up excuses for these blue cracks inside dementia where mercy conjures song and inside this blade-seared air, connect the letters, however briefly, one to another, and before another ambush, a short relief, a kiss blown into this hour.

THE MOON SOUNDS OF
EXPLODED FIRECRACKERS

Everybody has their own rebellion. —from *Andor*

1.

Your mother like
her mother before her
swore wishes plaited in suet
and bird seed.
Worn catalogs of
lessons never learned
lined the outskirts of their bodies
as they waded into futures
one hip at a time,
desire mocking their lips,
motion as mimetic device.

Promises whispered
in the dark after the children
went to bed with their ink-stained
futures laid out in patterns
of disappointments and triumphs
tucked into side pockets of suitcases
that nearly failed to leave.

Wrapped roundly
in her burial bones,
lessons lagged, voices

diminished by shoveling
salt, pain stenciled in their
knuckles, a flat swat
of dough slapped into shape
and baked to stave off hunger.

2.

I want to resemble a frame.
Or assemble a frame
or fit this sky of stars
flickering from my mouth
into a sentence.

Be real.

Maybe my mother
should have showed me
how far this orbit recedes
before it implodes and voices furl.

& what of your body covering
mine, cloaking these red scars?

Praise this calligraphy
where this breast's now ghosted
skyline is an amendment, a libretto
composed of spare epiphanies.

3.

I've been told it can take
seven years to finally say goodbye
to those we love and lose,
move scent into twiggy memory,
make it stick.
Yet even now, sometimes
I can coax a bright laugh
into this shifting point of view.

4.

Sometimes, hips ping.
Forests bloom
across nerve endings,
burn peripheral branches.

Maybe we should pack
up these little camps of loss,
and from this body
leave nothing behind but fire.

5.

Make a toast to moons
raveling on the outskirts of town.
To rice vibrating on the stove.

What a radical ear might make
of these drifting yet persistent noises
herding us forward, moving us
in choreographed frequencies,
where levitations of sound
suspend us in mid-air,
our feet barely touching
ground.   Forgiven.

As Upon a Raft

1.

When you leave,
heart loses her habit.
Crawl through darkness,
here, haiku takes its place
among tumbleweeds,
and red putty earth.
Each syllable, a bruised
trade, a scraped story
waiting to be clutched,
unspooled against
another desert sunset.

2.

We hope not to run
out of light outside
this all-too-familiar air.
Preferring, instead,
to pretend our panic
is a form of song
requiring scales that
only dogs can clearly hear.

3.

From the edge
of a bridge
into remember.
January is no
particular reason but
yes, here, again.
Your father's lone ceremony.
Stones over shut eyes.
Forgiveness in bitten minutia.

4.

Imagine touching a nerve.
Elegant pain.
Ask something irrevocably true.
Tumbleweeds are said to
be the first plant to grow
back after an apocalypse.

5.

When we drop the rain stick,
awe is loud & everywhere.
Rain conjures a sky
where there was none before.

For the Piano Man
Playing on the Side of the
Road During the Pandemic

Maybe we'll be okay,
someone will fill the potholes,
repair this frail horizon.
Hearts throw down rock
paper scissors, while another
road's miles dull one into another.

When we kiss this
shuttered world
goodnight,   it's a warbling
                    of birds
that spills into our ear
as if reading aloud our names.

And your mother, sudden
& alive again with her laugh,
hangs her hair over
the edge of a blue boat,
skims fingers over water
with what's left of her beauty
while your father,
another piano man,
lugs keys from town
to town on his back,
bewildered by his teeth, &

how in every photograph,
a future of his face
is laid bare,
lank and apparent to anyone
who understands history.

ALIVE

San Francisco Bay—For Brett

For instance, your felt hat,
found in a thrift store,
its brim slightly chewed,
could fail to stay

it could
fly down avenues

Even your father, his
history, moth-holed
almost laughs when
your urn refuses
             to sink under the waves.
        Nothing ends.
A handful of gray
ash fills our mouths as you
float the surface of this hour.

When we give in
      it's to an amnesia propped
up with soup cans,
freight and hollow of ordinary years,
an astonishment,   this scattering of fragile bonds.
To say I love you still,
and deliver us
from this humid world.

AFTER ALL STAY SOFT

While bombs dust dishes
and shoes, bodies and names
remain inscrutable,
another cautionary
tale gone sideways.

So give them our names.
Who knows one apple
from another?

In the dream,
I am pregnant but
too old to carry language
and so it goes.

Later, in the bar
there's frenzy
and a quiet corner.
Clocks have been removed,
calendars destroyed.
Motion hones motion.
We eat pancakes in the dark.
Forks hang mid-air,
potatoes and peas
hold the shape of the world.

How to Find Joy as a Common Object

From the journal of Elizabeth B., 1832

Like any physical exercise,
collecting seaweed
clears the head,
strengthens the body.
Or so I am told.   Mother
says it's a luxury
to own boots that allow
for climbing rocks unheeded.
To bury one self in sand
without retribution.

There are rules
to most everything
we do,   and this is no different—
from how to arrange
the pink undertow of kelp-lace
(before it decomposes)
to how high a petticoat
can rise before it provokes
and a throat is cleared.

Sometimes when I wake
it is the sea tangle
brine I pine for.
Its steps and blades.

Salt stiffening on my brow.
My brother is still alive
but now refuses to look
in my direction.

What will be told?
Memory, volatile and
at the same time inept,
(unkempt)   only knows itself and
what story can be transposed
as elegantly as seaweed?
Grapple the silvery finger
waving and changing perspective.
My mother, speechless, her hands
covering her mouth as if sound
could be construed as joy or jury.

When these boys' hunting boots,
too broad for my feet
refuse to hold this body steady,
I begin to see why
one must learn to kneel.

If I could be a small boat
and sail away.

One doesn't have to believe
in the presence of air
for it to fill our lungs.
Or misconstrue consent
as absolute to understand

that May, its pollen-sting
and swagger distilled,
will eventually be
out-numbered by June
brides and vows,
by mothers and brothers
standing ashore waving
goodbye to those who are
already gone.

AFTERTHOUGHT

Sarah Winchester kept
building to appease the dead.
What have you done lately?

One-way windows repeat their own
ghost stories in hallways
that fail to go anywhere
and brim with yellowed newspaper,
in memory of lost souls.

Cook swears he smells
curses lift from the flocked wallpaper,
cower deep in his nostrils.
Each waist-high syllable,
an unfixed hoodoo.
Pudding burns. Eggs weep.
Rifles scope and aim
toward a flock of crows
flinging seed at the ground's end.

The boy punts whatever is given.
Bird nests, a paper bag of ripe avocados
His own surprise jig into death.

If he could, he'd let Cook know
that the rifle that came for him
recognized its destination

and, the bullet,
weightless as a shrug,
yawned into his spine,
shuddering his knees.
As a matter of fact,
he told us he
didn't feel much.
Almost nothing at all.

HOW TO CROW

1.

To brim:
You must be a ghost in this
                story to make
its rambling work, to have a center
point to work from.   Rise up,
     know how to heft, to crow.   Fling your voice
into the future
              listen to how far its weight carries.

 See, nothing more
         than this inheritance
of tailspin and ashes is where we began.
Brothers, father, mother all jackknife
              & spill beauty.
Meanwhile, life craves another beginning,
rearranges atoms & dna.

                  For instance,
your soul might be
a courtyard of silence
and then BAM
crows come to babble
at your feet
preach their kicked-up seed
seek havoc, stir up shit

          &

2.

outside of reach
outside of line
time lifts it sweet skirt
disowns our common despair
        & sky brims untethered
from its earthly muffle.

3.

Ghosts in this
story might be insomniacs,
might be crows wading   belly-deep
in sky   hunting deer mice, voles
under a warm red moon.

Now, let's be clear,
crows will absolutely kill
if they can get their hands on even one.
& one is many. And many is (well you get the picture.)

4.

In this sentence
we love the soft sound of
our ordinary life. It slips
out of handcuffs with ease.

5.

Our first crow was a
loaded fairy tale but
also our provenance.

With a history that weighs
loss according to its pedigree
but also dances on furniture
we understand that every
consequence begs us to step lightly.

6.

It might be sweet salvation
that I need today but didn't know
until I found you here
in this ongoing history.

PEOPLE IN THIS COUNTRY

Stray out early enough
to discover crude flickers
of daylight between branches,
to be nervous witnesses—
Detonation converts conversation,
holds us captive in its reverb
What sort of distance
keeps this forest alive?
Breathing in the dark.
The birds don't know
which way to fly.
The news isn't good
and another sword
is pulled from its sheath,
left to ramble
an inevitable air.

Down the road
of errors, a story
will be cast off
and you'll be asked
to remember its source,
which weapons were used
and when the sky
lowered to catch
the refrain, how
late the hour was,
how lucky the dust.

How to Repair This Little Town

This world doesn't
belong to us
even as our bodies,   addled
break themselves open
quartz and shimmer
to a flaw.

What brings you here
to hero this little town
of faulty currents and feral cats?

Make mayonnaise sandwiches
for those wandering in
and out of doors even
as another house shifts
and falls away.

As branches
slap decks,
ruin avenues and stray dogs
limp over brown rocks
toward the only burning
homes they've
ever known.

Listen as vinyl and
needle skip over
another scratched bridge
trying to find a
way back to a beginning.

Never mind,
sew a running stitch
around this heart,
press the hole together
as if you understand
what it takes to go
on from here.

Festival

We don't have to decide
anything now.
No need to wrest choices,
or even take neutrality.
Instead, we can lift
the anchors from our skirts
and while homes drown
in their whirling coats
and animals scatter
to their festive ends,
we twirl,
make a feast,
a welcome for all.

About the Author

Michelle Murphy is the author of two previous poetry collections, *Jackknife & Light* (Avec Books) and *Synonym for Home* (Wet Cement Press). She lives with her husband and cat near the Truckee River in Reno, Nevada.